LET'S CREATE
ART

Fantastic art projects inspired by the works of the masters!

This edition published in 2013
By SpiceBox™
12171 Horseshoe Way
Richmond, BC
Canada V7A 4V4

First published in 2013
Copyright © SpiceBox™ 2013
Text and photographs copyright © Aladdin Books Ltd. 2001

ISBN 10: 1-77132-090-7
ISBN 13: 978-1-77132-090-0

CEO and Publisher: Ben Lotfi
Editorial: Ania Jaraczewski
Creative Director: Garett Chan
Art Director: Christine Covert
Design & Layout: Charmaine Muzyka
Production: James Badger, Mell D'Clute
Sourcing: Janny Lam, Desmond Hung

For more SpiceBox products and information, visit our website:
www.spiceboxbooks.com

Manufactured in China

1 3 5 7 9 10 8 6 4 2

Contents

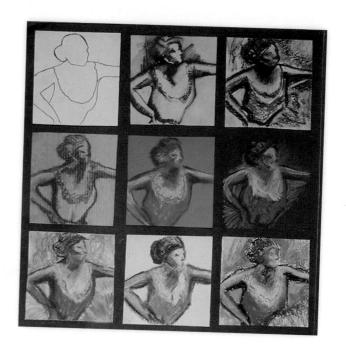

You don't have to be a brilliant artist to do the projects. Look at each piece of art, learn about the artists, and have fun being creative.

Introduction

Artists work with many different tools and materials to make art. They also spend a lot of time looking carefully at shapes, patterns, and colors in the world around them.

This book is about how artists see the world around them. On every page you will find a work of art by a different famous artist, which will give you ideas and inspiration for the project.

Working Like an Artist

It can help you in your work if you start by observing carefully and collecting ideas, just like an artist. Artists usually carry a sketchbook around with them all the time so they can put their ideas on paper immediately.

Words
You can take notes to remind you of the shapes, colors, and patterns you see.

Materials
Try different pencils, pens, paints, pastels, crayons, and materials to see what they do. Which would be best for this work?

Color
When you use color, mix all the colors you want first and try them out. It is amazing how many different shades you can make.

Using a Sketchbook

Before you start each project, this is the place to put your sketches. Try out your tools and materials, mix colors, and put in interesting papers and fabrics. You can then choose which ones you want to use.

Be a Magpie

Make a collection of things that interest you, like feathers, stones, or materials. Anything else that catches your eye could be useful in your artwork.

Art Box

You can collect tools and materials for your work and put them in a box. Sometimes you may need to go to an art store to get exactly what you need, but often you can find things that you can use at home. Ask for something for your art box for your birthday.

Chapter 1 - People

There are many ways to show people in your art. You can make a drawing or painting that looks just like the person. Or you can use all kinds of interesting materials to make them look silly or strange!

Klimt:
Pattern & Color
Klimt shows amazingly rich textures and patterns in his work. Make your own collage using many different materials. Pages 8–9

Degas: Drawing
Degas drew ballet dancers with chalks or pastels. Try using different materials and papers for different effects. Pages 16–17

Ravenna:
Making a Mosaic
Glass and stones were used in mosaics in Ravenna. You can make yours from paper. Pages 24–25

Arcimboldo:
Assemblage
Make a face in the style of Arcimboldo using any strange materials you can find. Pages 26–27

Drawing People

There are lots of methods artists use to make it easier to draw people. Look at the person you are drawing carefully, and make some practice sketches first.

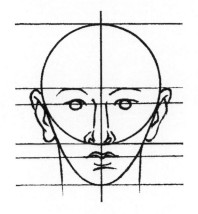

Head Shape

Look at the shape and draw the outline. Practice drawing eyes, noses, mouths, and ears in your sketchbook. How will you do the hair?

Face Measurements

It helps when drawing a face to divide the head into sections as shown above. See how the eyes sit on one line, and the nose on another. Look at where the ears and mouth are.

Body Measurements

About six heads fit into a full-length body. So, whatever size you draw the head, measure two more to the waist and three more to the feet. Always sketch first, and draw in the details afterward.

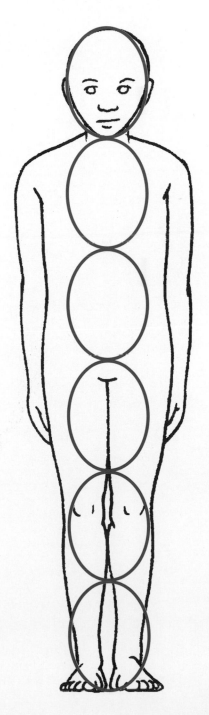

GALLERY

Look at the piece of art and think about:

The Kiss, 1908
Gustav Klimt (1862–1918)

Gold
Klimt's father made gold objects. Klimt used to watch him work and liked to make gold an important part of his own artwork.

Mosaic
After seeing mosaics in Italy, Klimt made this carpet of flowers look like a mosaic.

Model
The woman's face looks like the wife of one of Klimt's close friends.

Many people in Austria, where Gustav Klimt lived, thought he was an unusual and interesting artist. He was a big, quiet man who worked hard in his studio from early morning to late evening. All his paintings had a lot of pattern in them. He used straight lines for men and curved shapes for women. Hands interested him, and he often made them an important part of his pictures.

Pattern
Can you see the different types of pattern on the man's and woman's clothes?

Pattern & Color

What You Need:

- Cardboard
- Tape • Pen
- Colored tissue paper
- Candy wrappers
- Shiny paper
- Yarn • String
- Any fabrics, papers or other materials

You can make a figure using patterns and colors. Add some gold and silver paper, and paint, and make it in the style of Klimt. It would be fun to cover a life-sized picture in different fabrics, papers, and materials.

Project: A Life-sized Figure

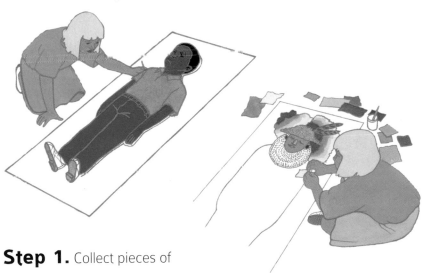

Step 1. Collect pieces of cardboard, and tape them together to make them as long as your friend. Draw around your friend with a pen. Use large pieces of bright-colored tissue paper to decorate the background.

Step 2. Look at Klimt's lovely patterns and shapes and copy some of them. Glue some candy wrappers or bright fabrics to make the clothes.

Step 3. You can use pictures of faces from magazines for the face. Yarn or string will make good hair.

GALLERY

Dancers in Yellow & Green, c. 1899–1904
Edgar Degas (1834–1917)

Impression
Degas did not show small details on hands and faces. He used pastels to create an impression of them.

Dots
Dots of yellow make the dancers' costumes come to life and shimmer in the light.

Background
Layers of pastels were built up on top of each other to make a lively background. Can you see that some of the marks are like scribbles?

Story
The dancers are all looking at something out of the picture. Perhaps they are waiting for their turn to go on stage.

Edgar Degas was born into a rich family in Paris. He studied art in Paris and Italy, and became a very skilled painter. He was one of the first artists to be interested in photography. He looked at people as if he were a camera, drawing them in action rather than posed as for a portrait.

Drawing

What You Need:

- Pastels
- Chalks
- Charcoals
- Pencils
- Wax crayons
- Felt-tip pens
- Paper scissors
- Tracing paper

Can you see how Degas used pastels to show the movement of the dancers and the light sparkling on their costumes? Degas liked to use different drawing materials in his pictures. You can try using different drawing materials and see what you can do with them.

Project: Materials

Step 1. Collect as many drawing materials and types of paper as possible. Cut the paper into squares. Make a viewfinder by folding a piece of paper into four. Cut out the middle and open it out. Pick a dancer from the picture, frame her in your viewfinder, and trace over her. Copy her on the pieces of paper.

Step 2. Use all your different drawing tools. Which ones make the dancer look most like the one Degas drew? Glue your drawings on a piece of cardboard to display them.

GALLERY

The Empress Theodora with Her Retinue, c. 547
Ravenna, Italy

Look at the piece of art and think about:

This mosaic is almost fifteen hundred years old. Many churches used mosaics to tell Bible stories. The artist for this mosaic is unknown, but the mosaics in Ravenna are probably the most famous in the world. This one shows the Roman Empress Theodora bringing gifts to the church.

Patterns
How many different patterns are there? They show how important the empress was.

Detail
Many pieces were used to create each face. They are so well done that from a distance they look like a painting.

Materials
Semiprecious stones were used in the mosaic to make Empress Theodora's beautiful jewelry.

Color
Look at the wonderfully rich colors used for this mosaic. Small pieces of bright glass were the main material used.

Making a Mosaic

What You Need:

- Magazines
- Pencil
- Cardboard
- Picture to copy
- Glue stick
- Brush
- Craft glue

Look at the colors, patterns, and tones in the mosaic from Ravenna in Italy. It was made by pressing pieces of colored glass, marble, and stone into cement to make a large picture. You can make your own mosaic using paper.

Project: Mosaic Portrait

Step 1. Find a picture in a magazine or a photo of a friend. Draw an outline of the face on a piece of cardboard.

Step 2. Cut or tear lots of colored scraps of paper from magazines. Choose colors that you can use to create a face, mouth, eyes, nose, and hair. Try to find lots of different tones of the same color.

Step 3. Glue the scraps to the cardboard to build up the face. When it is dry, paint over it with craft glue mixed with water as a varnish.

15

GALLERY

Vertumnus, 1590
Giuseppe Arcimboldo (1527–1593)

Detail
Each fruit and flower is painted with great care, showing every detail. Some look good enough to eat.

Fruit
Can you see why each piece of fruit has been chosen? The pear looks like the shape of a nose.

Subject
Do you find this man's head interesting, friendly, or a bit frightening?

Materials
What would you choose to make a head, eyes, nose, mouth, and hair if you were to make a picture like Arcimboldo's?

An Italian, born in 1527, Arcimboldo started his work as an artist by making stained-glass windows for churches. He became interested in painting strange and curious people who were considered grotesque. He painted fruit, flowers, trees, and vegetables to create his amazing heads.

Assemblage

What You Need:

- A collection of Interesting objects
- Cardboard
- Pencils
- Craft glue
- String

Many famous people liked Arcimboldo's portraits so much that they paid him to paint one for them. Arcimboldo's paintings are made by assembling a collection of objects. You can make a strange head using things you have at home.

Project: Collage

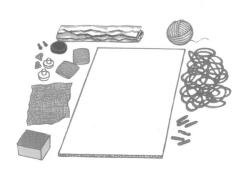

Step 1. Collect all kinds of interesting objects like paper clips, thread spools, string, nuts and bolts, hooks, screws, pins, wire, wrappers, and wood. Find a piece of cardboard from an old box. It will need to be thick and fairly big. Glue on some fine string to make the outline of a face and neck.

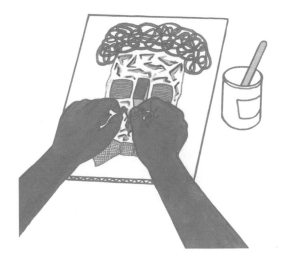

Step 2. Try out different objects you have collected to see which look best as eyes, ears, nose, and mouth. Choose something that would make good hair. When you have made your arrangement, glue it in place and let it dry. You could frame it and invite your friends to see your curious picture.

Chapter 2 - Landscapes

Look at all the different things you can see in a landscape scene. You might find fields, trees, mountains, lakes, houses, and more. What shape does each of these things have? First make a sketch to plan out your art before putting in the details.

Cézanne:
Composition & Color
See how Cézanne painted the foreground, middle ground, and background. You can do it, too! Pages 20–21

Gauguin:
Colors & Shapes
Gauguin used amazing colors and shapes. You can make a collage in the same style. Pages 22–23

Turner:
Seascapes
Turner liked to create a texture on his work. You can do this with tissue paper. Pages 24–25

Kandinsky:
Seeing Shapes
Kandinsky worked in paint. You can use his ideas about color and shape to make a textile collage. Pages 26–27

Drawing Landscapes

There are lots of things to think about when creating a landscape. Here are some tips that will help you improve your skills.

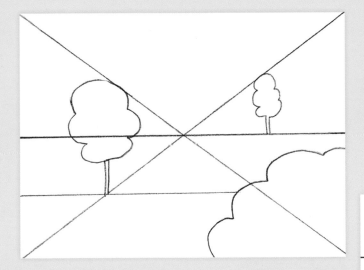

Composition

A landscape has things in the foreground, the middle ground, and the distance. Above is a simple grid that will help you with composition.

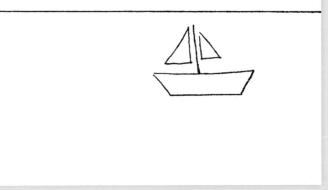

The horizon is where the earth or sea meets the sky in the distance. If you move the horizon line on a painting, you can make the same landscape or seascape look very different.

GALLERY

La Mer à L'Estaque, 1883–1886
Paul Cézanne (1839–1906)

Look at the piece of art and think about:

Paul Cézanne grew up in southern France. He was a shy, awkward young man who longed to be a painter. After working for a while in his father's bank, Cézanne went to Paris to become an artist. Through copying the work of famous artists, he taught himself to paint. Working outside was important to Cézanne, and he made up a new way of painting using blocks of color. Later he was called the "Father of Modern Art," because of his original style.

Distance
The foreground shows the most detail. Paler colors have been used to paint the sky and mountains. It makes them seem farther in the distance.

Composition
Look at how the painting is divided into three: the foreground, which is trees and land, the middle ground, which is the houses, and the ocean and mountains in the background.

Composition & Color

What You Need:

- Small box
- Paint • Pencil • Pens
- Paintbrushes
- Cardboard
- Watercolor paint
- Glue or tape
- Scissors

The way a picture is put together is called its composition. You can make the foreground and middle ground stand out from the background in a 3-D composition.

Project: 3-D Composition

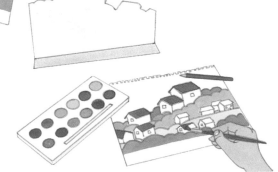

Step 1. Take a small box and paint an ocean on the bottom and halfway up the inside. The rest can be the sky. Look at Cézanne's painting to help you with colors.

Step 2. You may need help with this. Cut a piece of cardboard slightly smaller than the front of the box. Draw some houses and trees in pencil. Paint with watercolor. Cut around the top edge. Fold the bottom under and glue or tape it into the box halfway in.

Step 3. Make a frame for the front of the box and draw and paint trees on it. Glue it to the front of the box. You now have a 3-D painting.

GALLERY

Matamoe, 1892
Paul Gauguin (1848–1903)

Paul Gauguin led a colorful life like his many colorful paintings. He often worked with van Gogh and other famous painters. He left French society and traveled to the South Seas to fulfill himself as an artist. Gauguin thought that light, shape, and color were the most important part of paintings. You can see this in his work and in the moods that he creates in his paintings.

Look at the piece of art and think about:

Color
What mood do you think Gauguin was trying to show in this painting with the colors he used?

Shape
Look at the way Gauguin has made the shapes in his picture very simple.

Detail
How many things can you see that have been painted in their exact color?

Colors & Shapes

What You Need:

- Paint
- Paintbrush
- Cardboard
- Pencils
- Scissors
- Glue
- Paper

Gauguin used bright colors and simple shapes in his paintings. Look at a small part of Gauguin's painting and examine the colors and shapes he used. You can make a wonderful collage using the same style.

Project: Abstract Collage

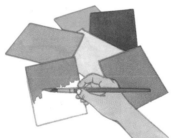

Step 1. Make a viewfinder by folding a piece of paper into four. Cut out the middle and open it out. Put it over the part of Gauguin's painting (opposite) that you like the best.

Step 2. Paint some pieces of thin cardboard with the colors you can see there and let them dry.

Step 3. Lightly draw each shape in your viewfinder onto the right color of cardboard and cut them out.

Step 4. Place the pieces onto a larger piece of cardboard. Glue them down when you are happy with the arrangement.

GALLERY

The *Sun of Venice* Setting Sail, 1843
J.M.W. Turner (1775–1851)

Look at the piece of art and think about:

The first drawings Turner did were put in the window of his father's barbershop in Covent Garden, London. At 14 he began to study art seriously and had his first picture in an art gallery when he was 17. As he traveled around England and Europe, he filled hundreds of sketchbooks with wonderful drawings and sketches, which he later turned into paintings.

Contrast
The darker ripples of the sea contrast with the white and yellow sky.

Palette Knife
Instead of using a brush, Turner used a small, flat knife to spread the oil paint on the canvas.

Poetry
This painting tells a sad story Turner read in a poem. It was about a fishing boat leaving Venice, never to return because of storms.

Seascapes

What You Need:

- Tissue paper
- Cardboard
- Glue
- Water
- Paints
- Paintbrush

Turner used white with oil to make his paint look almost transparent. He also liked to create a texture on the surface. If you use glue, tissue paper, and paint, you can get a transparent, textured effect to your work.

Project: Mixed Media

Step 1. Put some glue on the cardboard. Crease and crumple some plain tissue paper and lay it on the cardboard. Paint more glue over the textured surface and leave it to dry.

Step 2. Mix different yellow, red, orange, and white colors for a sea picture. Use a big, soft brush to paint on top of the tissue paper making waves and swirls of water. Use lots of different shades like Turner. Let them blend into each other.

GALLERY

Landscape with Church, 1909
Wassily Kandinsky (1866–1944)

Look at the piece of art and think about:

Dr. Wassily Kandinsky was all set to become a university professor in Russia when he decided he wanted to study art. He went on to paint in many different and exciting modern styles. He loved modern music and thought that as different sounds made a whole piece of music, so different colors and shapes can come together to make a painting.

Focal Point
An important part of a painting that draws your eye is called the focal point. What do you think is the focal point of this picture?

Friendship
Kandinsky did many paintings while he was staying at his friend's vacation home at Murnau.

Color
This landscape is painted in patches of bright color. How many different colors can you see? Each color plays an important part in creating an atmosphere or mood in this work of art.

Seeing Shapes

What You Need:

- Colored felt
- Needle • Glue
- Selection of material
- Scissors
- Selection of thread
- Large piece of heavy fabric

Kandinsky worked in paint. He used large areas of solid color to make shapes. You can use the same ideas to make a textile landscape. Choose bright colors like the ones in the Murnau landscape, and glue and stitch them to some material.

Project: Textiles

Step 1. Collect some brightly colored material. You need a large piece of heavy fabric as a background. Cut out some shapes like the ones in Kandinsky's painting.

Step 2. Arrange your material on the background to make a picture. Glue the pieces in place. Once the glue has dried, add some stitches to the materials in colored thread for small interesting features like stars, leaves, or windows.

Chapter 3 - Sports & Leisure

In the past, before television, computers, and movies, people had very different ways of spending their leisure time. They would go on picnics, sit in cafés, or perhaps go on boat trips. You can see this in their paintings.

Münter:
Expressionist Boat Trip

Münter used simple shapes and colors. Try making a collage using her style. Pages 30–31

Brueghel:
Detailed Ice Skaters

Brueghel painted a winter sporting scene in detail. You can make a snowy collage. Pages 32–33

Gauguin:
Painted Horse Riders

Gauguin painted horse riders galloping along a beach. You can make a 3-D scene of horses and riders. Pages 34–35

Drawing Sporting Figures

Paintings often show people doing activities they enjoy. What kinds of sports and games do you do in your free time? Pick something you like and use it as the subject for your next artwork!

Body Shapes

Start by drawing simple shapes to show the head, arms, and legs. Look at how the body is made up.

Try to break the body down into easy lines. Think of the shoulders as one line, the arms and legs as others.

Make sure you have made the head the right size, and check that the legs are not too long or too short.

Look at where the joints are and how they move.

Once you have mastered this and the proportions look right, try drawing a different pose using the same technique.

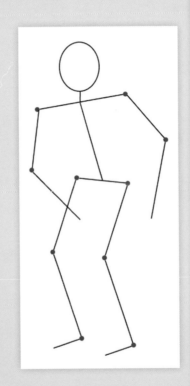

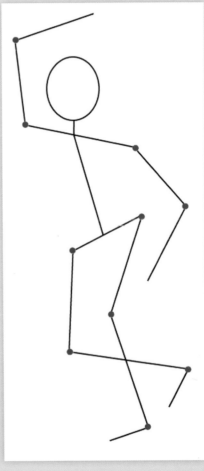

GALLERY

Boat Trip, 1910
Gabriele Münter (1877–1962)

Shape
Münter liked to change what she saw into simpler shapes and colors.

Composition
The arrangement of people, background, colors, and shapes cleverly draws your eye around the picture.

People
A group of Expressionist artists used to go on vacation together each year to paint. Could this be the artists on a boat trip?

Feeling
How does this picture make you feel? Do you think Münter liked boat trips?

When Gabriele Münter started painting in Germany, women were not allowed to put their pictures into art exhibitions with men. They were expected to stay at home and look after their families. But Gabriele spent her life painting. She particularly liked painting people. She said her work was about "self-expression," and she became a member of the Expressionist group of painters.

Expressionist Boat Trip

What You Need:

- Selection of paper and cardboard
- Fabrics
- Pencil
- Paper
- Scissors
- Glue

The colors and shapes used by Gabriele Münter are very pleasing to the eye and can easily be turned into a collage. If you draw, cut, and paste together some simple shapes cut from cardboard or fabrics, you can make a boating scene of your own.

Project: Boating Collage

Step 1. Draw your picture of a boating scene onto cardboard using simple shapes. Collect different papers and fabrics that are good colors for your scene.

Step 2. Cut out mountains, fields, and water shapes for the background and water. Arrange them on the cardboard. Add a boat and people.

Step 3. When you are happy with the arrangement, glue everything in place.

GALLERY

Winter, 1622–1635
Pieter Brueghel (1564–1638)

Look at the piece of art and think about:

In Holland during the winter, the canals and rivers used to freeze over, and people enjoyed skating on them. Pieter Brueghel painted many scenes of children and adults spending time together having fun.

Distance
The people in the front (foreground) are much bigger than those people in the distance. Yet they are all carefully painted.

Activities
How many different activities can you see going on? Did you spot a man who had fallen into the river?

Detailed Ice Skaters

What You Need:

- Blunt knife • Paints
- Styrofoam • Glue
- Felt-tip pen • Sponge
- Shiny paper • Twigs
- Wire / pipe cleaners
- Used matchstick
- Paintbrush

Pieter Brueghel was one of a large family of painters. He often painted cool, wintery scenes with people enjoying the ice and snow. Look for some packaging materials that could make a collage of a snowy scene. Make sure they are cool colors.

Project: Snow & Ice Collage

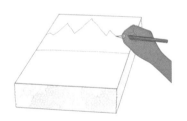

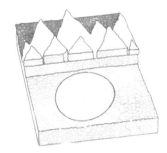

Step 1. Ask an adult to help you to cut out a square from Styrofoam packaging and draw mountains and a lake area on it in felt pen.

Step 2. Get an adult to help you cut away the Styrofoam to make the mountains and lake shapes. Use a blunt knife very carefully. Paint the sky blue and add some of the cut-out mountain shapes to make more mountains. Glue a piece of shiny paper for a pond.

Step 3. The figures can be made from wire or pipe cleaners. Add skates to the feet by painting a used matchstick black and cutting it in four. Green sponge and twigs will make trees. Glue everything on to complete your picture.

GALLERY

Riders on the Beach, 1902
Paul Gauguin (1848–1903)

Look at the piece of art and think about:

Paul Gauguin was born in Paris. However, he left his family and career in France to spend much of his life on the South Sea island of Tahiti. He hated city life and enjoyed living a simple life close to nature. Many of his paintings were of the tropical forests and beaches, where he loved the freedom of riding a horse. The warm colors he used show the enjoyment he had in his way of life.

Feeling
How does the painting make you feel? How do you think Gauguin felt when he painted it?

Time of Day
The warm but soft colors could be the early morning or evening light on the beach.

Brush Strokes
Gauguin has used different kinds of brush strokes to blend colors together for the sky, sea, and sand.

Freedom
The figures are not wearing many clothes and are riding their horses bareback.

Painted Horse Riders

What You Need:

- Stiff cardboard
- Paint
- Paintbrushes
- Pencils
- Scissors
- Cardboard
- Glue

Many people enjoy riding along a beach like the figures in Gauguin's painting. They almost look as though they could jump out of the back of the picture. A 3-D effect can be achieved by cutting out horses and riders and adding them to a background.

Project: 3-D Horse Riders

Step 1. Paint a beach background on cardboard. Draw some horses and riders on another piece of cardboard. Paint them in warm colors. Use Gauguin's picture to help you choose shapes and colors.

Step 2. Cut out the horses and riders. Fold two pieces of paper as shown and glue one to the back of each horse.

Step 3. Glue the other end of the folded cardboard to the background to finish the picture.

Chapter 4 - Still Life

Even the most ordinary objects can become the inspiration for great works of art. With still life, you can create your own scene to copy any way you like.

Redon: Painting Flowers

Redon painted some wonderful flowers. You can use a sponge to put the paint on your work. Pages 38–39

Gauguin:
Sculpting Fruit

See how Gauguin made fruit look three-dimensional. You can make 3-D fruit from newspaper. Pages 40–41

Van Gogh: Working in 3-D

Van Gogh's bedroom is famous because he painted it. You can make his bedroom in 3-D. Pages 42–43

Drawing Still Life Objects

You can make a still life arrangement out of things you find around your home. Then try out these tips for practice.

You may sometimes find that what you draw looks flat. Shading is a useful way of making things you draw look three-dimensional. Experiment with shading in your sketchbook.

Try to arrange some objects at home into a good composition. Don't just put the objects in a line, put some things at the front and some at the back. Look at what you have done and rearrange it until you are happy with it.

GALLERY

Flowers in a Turquoise-Colored Vase, c. 1905
Odilon Redon (1840–1916)

Look at the piece of art and think about:

Background
The colors of the flowers stand out against the background.

Vase
This vase catches your eye, too, with its bright color.

Materials
Can you see brush strokes or other marks on the painting? What do you think Redon used to paint the flowers? Look at the texture of the leaves and the petals.

Odilon Redon was often sick as a child. He became very shy and liked to hide away from people as he grew up. He did not want to be an artist like the Impressionists. He used his imagination to make black and white prints and charcoal drawings. Later in his life he found happiness with his wife and friends and began to use color. He said, "Color contains joy."

Painting Flowers

What You Need:

- Flowers
- Sponge paper
- Paint
- Pastels
- Hairspray
- Paintbrushes
- Colored paper

Many artists including Odilon Redon have enjoyed painting flowers. Get some flowers from the garden or a florist and try out different printing and painting methods to make a colorful picture.

Project: Mixed Media Flowers

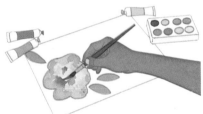

Step 1. Look carefully at the flowers you have in front of you. You could paint each flower using a different method. Start with a piece of sponge to print the petals and leaves in different colors.

Step 2. Paintbrushes and fingers can be used to dab extra colors and shapes onto the flowers.

Step 3. When the paint has dried, add some pastel marks and small pieces of colored paper to give texture. You can spray it with hairspray to stop it from smudging.

GALLERY

Look at the piece of art and think about:

Still Life with Profile of Laval, 1886
Paul Gauguin (1848–1903)

Brush
Gauguin has used a large brush and loose strokes to paint his still life.

Objects
What other objects can you see on the table that Laval is looking at?

Composition
Laval looking at the fruit draws your eye in to look at it, too.

3-D Effect
See how shadows, tones, and highlights make the fruit look three-dimensional

Until the age of six, Paul Gauguin lived with his parents in Peru, South America. The colors, smells, and way of life stayed with him and he always longed to return. In 1883 he decided to become a painter and traveler. Later he lived abroad and painted using very bright colors.

Sculpting Fruit

What You Need:

- Newspaper
- Glue
- Water
- Paint
- Tape
- Paintbrush

Gauguin has painted the fruit in this still life to look three-dimensional. You can make 3-D fruit by using paper and glue. The pieces of fruit could then be arranged into a still life.

Project: 3-D Fruit

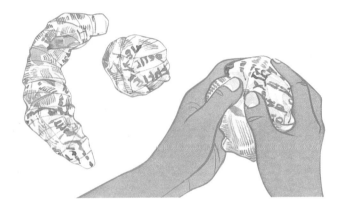

Step 1. Scrunch used newspaper into the shape of different fruit. Tape it together.

Step 2. Dip strips of newspaper into a mixture of glue and water. Wrap around the fruit. Leave it to dry.

Step 3. Paint each piece of fruit to look as real as possible.

Step 4. When the paint is dry, arrange your fruit into a still life.

GALLERY

Vincent's Bedroom at Arles, 1889
Vincent van Gogh 1853–1890

Look at the piece of art and think about:

Throughout his life van Gogh was poor, often hungry, and ill. This is the bedroom in the house he shared with Paul Gauguin. The two artists worked together and they often argued as well, especially about who should clean the house. This painting shows how neat van Gogh could be, and is a record of how he lived.

Shadows
There are no shadows in the room as the shutters are closed, keeping out the light.

Brush Strokes
These thick brush strokes look just like a wooden floor.

Working in 3-D

What You Need:

- Scissors
- Shoebox
- Paint
- Paintbrush
- Cardboard
- Glue

Van Gogh lived a simple life, but his room looks attractive with its bright colors. You can bring van Gogh's bedroom to life by making it in cardboard in three dimensions. When you have done that, you could also make a 3-D picture of your own room. Remember to clean it up first!

Project: 3-D Bedroom

Step 1. Cut the front off an old shoebox or other small box. Paint the walls and floor to look like van Gogh's bedroom.

Step 2. Make a bed and chairs out of cardboard. Make sure they fit into the box. Paint them the same colors van Gogh used.

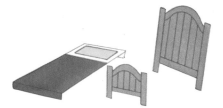

Step 3. When the furniture is dry, fold the bottom of the legs under. Arrange them in the shoebox room, and when you are happy with their positions, glue them to the floor of the box.

Chapter 5 - Animals

Draw a picture of your pet, or find a photo of an animal to copy in a book or magazine. Look at all kinds of animals to see how each is different. Pay attention to details like fur, feathers, scales, claws, teeth, and horns.

Mosaic at Pompeii:
Roman Mosaic

The Romans made mosaics from stones and tiles. You can make one from beans. Pages 46–47

Cave Painting at Lascaux: Cave Art

Long ago, people painted animals on cave walls. Make your own wall art. Pages 48–49

Rousseau:
Jungle Painting

Rousseau liked to paint animals in jungles. Make a jungle collage, and hide an animal in it! Pages 52–53

Franz Marc:
Expressionism

Look at the wonderful colors Franz Marc used to paint his horses. Make your own animal print with bright colors. Pages 50–51

Raphaël: imagination

Raphael painted a wonderful dragon. Use your imagination to create your own fierce creature. Pages 54–55

Drawing Animals

Animals come in all shapes and sizes. Artists draw animals by starting from the largest shapes first, and then putting in details.

Body Shapes

Start by drawing simple shapes to show the head, body, legs, tail, and ears.

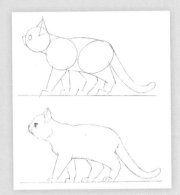

Proportion

Make sure you have made the head the right size, and check that the legs are not too long or too short.

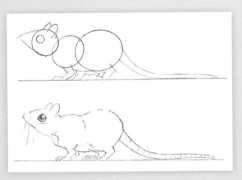

Fur, Hair & Skin

Does the animal have fur, hair, skin, or unusual colors? Find out how you will draw them by trying out some ideas in your sketchbook.

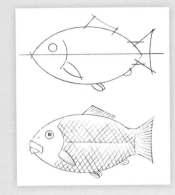

Finishing Touches

Once you have the size and shapes right, you can start to fill in the details and add color.

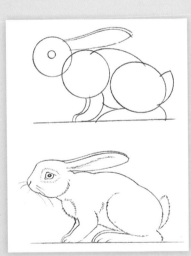

GALLERY

Beware of the Dog, AD 79
Pompeii Mosaic

Look at the piece of art and think about:

Materials
Mosaics were usually made from many small, colored stones, tiles, or marble. This one was made from marble pieces.

Warning
The dog looks as fierce as the artist could make it, to scare people away.

Colors
Marble is never found in very bright colors, so the tones used for this dog are natural: red, white, and gray.

Decoration
Mosaics were used to decorate palaces and churches in ancient times.

This mosaic was discovered in the remains of Pompeii long after Mount Vesuvius had erupted in AD 79. It was probably made to lie in the sidewalk outside a wealthy person's house. It would have acted as a warning to passersby to beware of the dog; it would also warn thieves to keep away!

Roman Mosaic

What You Need:

- Cardboard
- Pencil
- Picture to copy
- Selection of beans and lentils
- Craft glue

Mosaics were used by the Romans to decorate walls, floors, and pavements. This dog was found in Pompeii, Italy. It is a warning sign saying, "Beware of the Dog." Why not make your own mosaic of your pet or any interesting animal?

Project: Pet Mosaic

Step 1. Draw a simple outline of your animal on cardboard. Use a photograph or picture from a magazine or book to help you.

Step 2. Collect dried beans, lentils, and peas in different colors. Spread craft glue onto the cardboard and stick them on to make your animal.

GALLERY

Horse, 17,000 BC
Lascaux Cave Painting

Look at the piece of art and think about:

This horse is part of a 100-foot-long gallery of prehistoric cave paintings at Lascaux in France. The only colors used were made from powdered rock and soil. White, green, and blue were not used because they could not be made. The paintings were often made in dark caves, and this helped to protect them so that we can still see them today.

Eye
Which way do you think this horse is looking? Perhaps it is wondering what will be coming up behind it.

Surface
Look carefully at the surface of the painting. You can tell that it has been drawn on a rock wall. Can you see the cracks, scratches, and marks there?

Magic
Ancient people were often afraid of things they did not understand. They thought their paintings made a magic that would help them.

Line
It is easy to see the outline of this horse even though it is very old. The artist would have used a sharpened stick dipped in dark earth.

Cave Art

What You Need:

- Oil pastels
- Charcoal pencil
- Sketchbook
- Pencil
- Thick cardboard
- Acrylic paints
- Sand

Long ago, people painted the walls of caves with pictures of animals and sometimes people. The paintings were probably thought of as magic and were painted in special places away from where people lived.

Project: Wall Drawing

Step 1. Find a piece of thick cardboard. Mix some sand with white and pale yellow acrylic paint. Cover the cardboard with the paint to make it look like the wall of a cave.

Step 2. Sketch some outlines of animals in your sketchbook. Copy two or three onto your homemade wall, using a black oil pastel or charcoal pencil.

Step 3. Shade each animal with yellow and reddish brown, which were the colors used by cave artists.

GALLERY

Blue Horse 1, 1911
Franz Marc (1880–1916)

Look at the piece of art and think about:

Color

Marc used colors in his paintings that did not clash but made the picture feel calm. He painted the world through the eyes of an animal. Here you see how Marc thought a horse saw the world it lived in.

The best paintings of Franz Marc's were done toward the end of his life. He thought each color had a mood of its own, and he wanted the color to draw people into the feelings in his painting. He was not interested in painting a realistic picture.

Brush Strokes

You can see that Marc used sweeping brush strokes to paint the landscape and the horse's body.

Expressionism

What You Need:

- Craft glue
- Pencil
- Paints
- Paintbrush
- White cardboard
- Paper

It was important to Franz Marc that he paint animals and their world as if he were looking through their eyes. He used colors that expressed a feeling rather than being exactly like the animal or landscape. A print can do this, too.

Project: Horse Prints

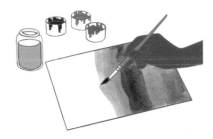

Step 1. Make some green, blue, red, and yellow watery paints. Use a thick brush and spread the different colors over a piece of white cardboard.

Step 2. Draw an outline of your favorite animal. If you choose to do a horse use Marc's picture to help you.

Step 3. Draw over the outline with craft glue using a container with a nozzle. Leave the glue to dry.

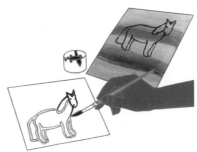

Step 4. Paint over the glue outline with dark paint. Press it onto a piece of spare paper to test it first. When you are ready, print one or two animals onto the cardboard you painted earlier.

GALLERY

Exotic Landscape With Tiger, 1907
Henri Rousseau (1844–1910)

Look at the piece of art and think about:

Leaves
How many different leaf shapes can you see? Rousseau studied tropical plants in Paris so he could paint them.

When he retired from an office job, Henri Rousseau began to paint. He taught himself, and to his surprise soon became famous. Picasso liked his paintings and gave Rousseau a big party to celebrate his work. For this jungle painting, Henri Rousseau went to a zoo in Paris to study the tigers.

Color
The main color used by Rousseau is green. What effect does this have on the other colors he has used?

Camouflage
Is it easy or difficult to see the tiger among the leaves? What is the tiger hiding from?

Animals
There are two other animals watching and waiting to see what will happen. Can you see them?

Jungle Painting

What You Need:

- Glue
- Pencil
- Magazines
- Paper
- Chalk
- Pastels
- Scissors

Rousseau liked to paint animals in jungles with large leaves and colorful flowers. You can put a tiger in a jungle by cutting shapes out of scrap magazines and hiding the tiger behind them.

Project: Tiger Collage

Step 1. Draw a tiger and color it with chalk pastels. Cut it out.

Step 2. Collect gold, green, and brown colors from magazines. Cut out leaf and tree shapes. You can make some colorful flowers, too.

Step 3. Put the tiger onto a dark background and arrange the leaf, tree, and flower shapes around and on top of the tiger. Make sure you can still see it!

Step 4. Glue the shapes on when you like the arrangement. You have made a jungle collage.

GALLERY

St. George Fighting With The Dragon, c. 1505
Raphael (1483–1520)

Woman
St. George has rescued this woman from the evil dragon. Can you see how Raphael has made her look soft and delicate?

Distance
The dragon and St. George stand out, while the background fades into the distance in pale blues and greens.

Horse
Why do you think the horse is white? It certainly stands out in the center of the painting.

Dragon
Raphael used different tones of black and white to make the dragon's skin shine and gleam in an evil way.

When Raphael was eleven, his father died. He then went to work in a studio to learn to become a painter. He became one of Italy's most famous artists. Best of all, he liked to paint the Holy Family and saints. In this painting he is showing how good overcomes evil, from the popular story of St. George saving the young woman from the terrors of the dragon.

Imagination

What You Need:

- Scissors • Brush
- Cardboard
- Acrylic paint
- Pencils • Chalk
- Any interesting, bright things
- Craft glue

Raphael's painting tells the story of St. George fighting the dragon. Raphael used his imagination to make his dragon. He has made it look very wicked and dark. You can make a mixed media dragon that looks lively and colorful.

Project: Mixed Media Dragon

Step 1. Draw the outline of an imaginary dragon on dark cardboard with a light chalk or pencil line.

Step 2. Paint in the patterns and shapes on the dragon's skin, wings, and face. Paint a bright color around the outline of the whole dragon.

Step 3. Cut up some silver, gold, and shiny paper and stick it onto the dragon. Sequins, buttons, shiny wrapping paper, and thread can be added, until you have a very bold dragon.